WOMEN
LEADING
THE WAY

Maria Tallchief
Prima Ballerina

by Kate Moening

BELLWETHER MEDIA • MINNEAPOLIS, MN

Blastoff! Readers are carefully developed by literacy experts to build reading stamina and move students toward fluency by combining standards-based content with developmentally appropriate text.

Level 1 provides the most support through repetition of high-frequency words, light text, predictable sentence patterns, and strong visual support.

Level 2 offers early readers a bit more challenge through varied sentences, increased text load, and text-supportive special features.

Level 3 advances early-fluent readers toward fluency through increased text load, less reliance on photos, advancing concepts, longer sentences, and more complex special features.

★ **Blastoff! Universe**

Reading Level

Grade **K**

Grades **1–3**

Grade **4**

This edition first published in 2021 by Bellwether Media, Inc.

No part of this publication may be reproduced in whole or in part without written permission of the publisher. For information regarding permission, write to Bellwether Media, Inc., Attention: Permissions Department, 6012 Blue Circle Drive, Minnetonka, MN 55343.

Library of Congress Cataloging-in-Publication Data

Names: Moening, Kate, author.
Title: Maria Tallchief : prima ballerina / by Kate Moening.
Description: Minneapolis, MN : Bellwether Media, Inc., [2021] | Series: Blastoff! readers : Women leading the way | Includes bibliographical references and index. | Audience: Ages 5-8 | Audience: Grades K-1 | Summary: "Relevant images match informative text in this introduction to Maria Tallchief. Intended for students in kindergarten through third grade"– Provided by publisher.
Identifiers: LCCN 2019053738 (print) | LCCN 2019053739 (ebook) | ISBN 9781644872109 (library binding) | ISBN 9781681038346 (paperback) | ISBN 9781618919687 (ebook)
Subjects: LCSH: Tallchief, Maria–Juvenile literature. | Indian ballerinas–United States–Biography–Juvenile literature. | Ballerinas–United States–Biography–Juvenile literature. | Osage Indians–United States–Biography–Juvenile literature.
Classification: LCC GV1785.T32 M64 2021 (print) | LCC GV1785.T32 (ebook) | DDC 792.8092 [B]–dc23
LC record available at https://lccn.loc.gov/2019053738
LC ebook record available at https://lccn.loc.gov/2019053739

Text copyright © 2021 by Bellwether Media, Inc. BLASTOFF! READERS and associated logos are trademarks and/or registered trademarks of Bellwether Media, Inc.

Editor: Elizabeth Neuenfeldt   Designer: Andrea Schneider

Printed in the United States of America, North Mankato, MN.

Table of Contents

Who Was Maria Tallchief?

Maria Tallchief was a world-famous **prima ballerina**. She was the first Native American prima ballerina!

Maria was known for her graceful skill and **energy**.

"I WANTED TO BE [RESPECTED] AS A PRIMA BALLERINA WHO HAPPENED TO BE A NATIVE AMERICAN." (1997)

Maria grew up in Oklahoma. She belonged to the **Osage Nation**.

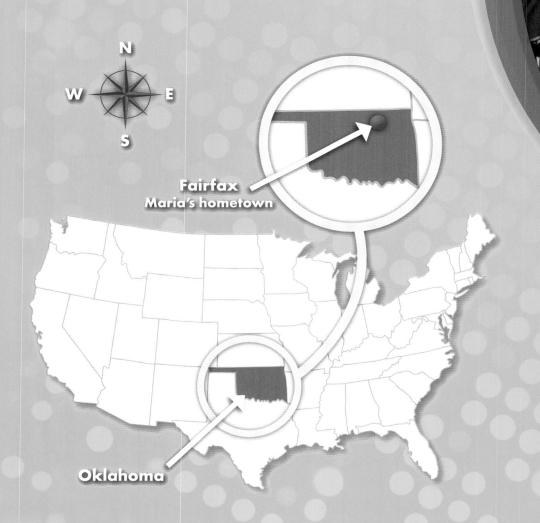

Fairfax
Maria's hometown

Oklahoma

members of the
Osage Nation

Maria started dance lessons
at a young age.

Getting Her Start

Maria with her family

When Maria was 8, her family moved to California. She joined a better dance school.

Maria was shy and serious. Dance helped her find her voice!

Maria Tallchief Profile

Birthday: January 24, 1925

Hometown: Fairfax, Oklahoma

Field: dance

Schooling: high school

Influences:
- Bronislava Nijinska (dance teacher)
- Mia Slavenska (ballet dancer)
- Alexandra Danilova (ballet dancer)
- George Balanchine (choreographer, teacher, and husband for six years)

After high school,
Maria moved to
New York City.
She was only 17.

She wanted to join
a **ballet company**!

New York City

Maria struggled to find work. Most companies only wanted white dancers.

People said her name sounded too Native American. Maria refused to change it. She was proud of her **heritage**!

Finally, a company chose Maria as an **understudy**. Soon she **performed** lead parts.

Maria traveled to many countries. People everywhere loved Maria's dancing!

Maria in London

"[THE ART] IS WHAT IT IS ALL ABOUT.... IN EVERY SENSE OF THE WORD **YOU ARE POETRY IN MOTION.**" (1994)

In 1954, Maria became prima ballerina. Many dances were **choreographed** just for her.

Maria in *The Nutcracker*

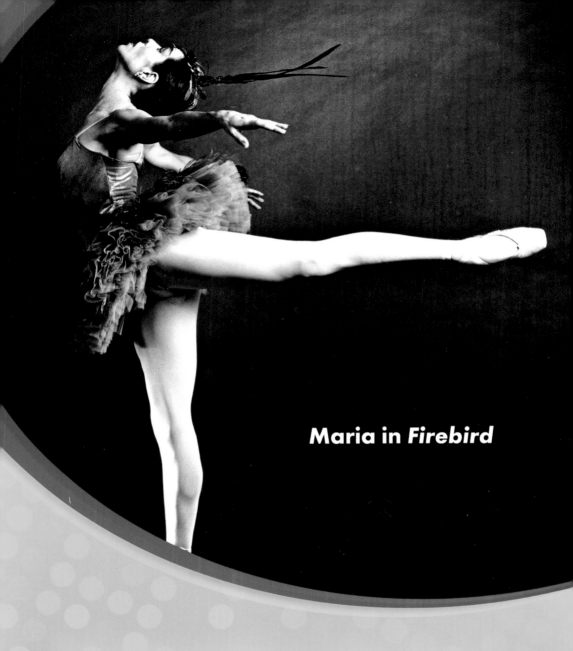

Maria in *Firebird*

Maria's most famous show was called *Firebird*. She made the New York City Ballet famous!

Maria's Legacy

Maria stopped performing in 1965. She wanted to teach younger dancers.

Maria started a dance
school in Chicago.
Her students loved her!

Maria Tallchief Timeline

1942	Maria moves to New York City and joins her first ballet company
1954	Maria is named prima ballerina of the New York City Ballet
1965	Maria stops performing and begins teaching
1981	Maria and her sister start Chicago City Ballet
1999	Maria is awarded the American National Medal of the Arts

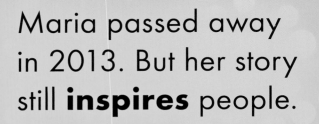

Maria passed away in 2013. But her story still **inspires** people.

Most ballet dancers are still white. But Maria shows people of all **backgrounds** can become dancers!

"YOU CAN DANCE TO ANYTHING." (1994)

Glossary

backgrounds—people's experiences, knowledge, and family histories

ballet company—a group of people who work together to put on a ballet performance

choreographed—decided how a dancer or group of dancers should move during a performance

energy—power and strength

heritage—the traditions and beliefs that are a part of the history of a group of people or nation

inspires—gives someone an idea about what to do or create

Osage Nation—a Native American group; the Osage homeland was in what is now Arkansas, Missouri, Kansas, and Texas.

performed—did an action or activity that required training and skill

prima ballerina—the highest-ranking female dancer in a ballet company; the prima ballerina performs the lead parts.

understudy—a dancer who prepares to take the part of another dancer if that dancer is unable to perform

To Learn More

AT THE LIBRARY

Bowes, Deborah. *The Ballet Book: The Young Performer's Guide to Classical Dance*. Buffalo, N.Y.: Firefly Books, 2018.

Clinton, Chelsea. *She Persisted: 13 American Women Who Changed the World*. New York, N.Y.: Philomel Books, 2017.

Moening, Kate. *Ava DuVernay: Movie Director*. Minneapolis, Minn.: Bellwether Media, 2021.

ON THE WEB

FACTSURFER

Factsurfer.com gives you a safe, fun way to find more information.

1. Go to www.factsurfer.com.

2. Enter "Maria Tallchief" into the search box and click 🔍.

3. Select your book cover to see a list of related content.

Index

The images in this book are reproduced through the courtesy of: Donaldson Collection/ Contributor/ Getty Images, front cover (Maria); Allaganskaia, front cover, pp. 3, 23; Nagel Photography, front cover (theater); Jack Mitchell/ Contributor/ Getty Images, pp. 4 (inset), 4-5, 9, 16-17 (top); FPG/ Staff/ Getty Images, pp. 6-7; A. Y. Owen/ Contributor/ Getty Images, pp. 8-9 (top); Atanas Bezov, p. 10 (inset); The Washington Post/ Contributor/ Getty Images, pp. 10-11; Paul Popper/ Popperfoto/ Contributor/ Getty Images, pp. 12-13 (top); Martha Holmes/ Contributor/ Getty Images, p. 13; Mirrorpix/ Contributor/ Getty Images, p. 14 (inset); Keystone/ Stringer/ Getty Images, pp. 14-15; Alfred Eisenstaedt/ Contributor/ Getty Images, p. 16; Bettmann/ Contributor/ Getty Images, pp. 18-19; CREATISTA, p. 20 (inset); Stacia Timonere/ Contributor/ Getty Images, pp. 20-21.